SEBASTIAN IN EGYPT

By M.C. Hall
Illustrated by David T. Wenzel

Published by Bear & Company Publications

Printed in the United States of America

Based on a series concept by Dawn Jones
Edited by Dawn Jones
Designed by Valerie Hodgson

Library of Congress Cataloging-in-Publication Data

Hall, Margaret, 1947-
Sebastian in Egypt / written by M.C. Hall ; illustrated by David T. Wenzel.
p. cm. – (Suitcase bear adventures)
"Based on a series concept by Dawn Jones."
Summary: On a trip to Egypt with his human family, a teddy bear with dreams of making his way into history books gets into mischief instead.
ISBN 0-9713174-2-9 (alk. paper)
[1. Teddy bears–Fiction. 2. Behavior–Fiction. 3. Egypt–Fiction.] I. Wenzel, David T., 1950- ill. II. Jones, Dawn L., 1963- III. Title. IV. Series.
PZ7.H14625 Si 2001
[Fic]–dc21
2001005171

To Jason, who is a lot like Sebastian

M. C. *Hall*

Message to Parents

Bear & Company, part of The Boyds Collection, Ltd. family, is committed to creating quality reading and play experiences that inspire kids to learn, imagine, and explore the world around them. Working together with experienced children's authors, illustrators, and educators, we promise to create stories and products that are respectful to your children and that will earn your respect in turn.

Table of Contents

Chapter One
Going in Circles

"My suitcase!" cried Sebastian.

"Wait!" Emily called. "I'll get it for you!"

"I can get it," Sebastian muttered as he ran alongside the moving luggage belt. He was crabby. It had been a long trip to Egypt. He was tired of sitting. He was tired of airplanes. He was tired of airports.

Sebastian reached out and grabbed the handle of his suitcase. Whoosh! He was whisked through the air and up onto the moving belt. He heard Emily cry out: "Sebastian!"

The belt kept going. Then–

Flap! Slap! Strips of plastic smacked against Sebastian's head. He closed his eyes as he was carried into a dark tunnel.

Where am I? he wondered. *Will I end up in the Lost and Found?*

Sebastian thought about Ms. Valentine. Going to the Lost and Found wasn't on her schedule. She wouldn't be happy–especially since she had told Emily to leave him at home. "Everywhere we go, that bear causes problems," she had said.

However, Sebastian went everywhere with nine-year-old Emily and her little brother, Ben, who was seven. Mr. and Mrs. Parker, the children's parents, traveled all over the world. They liked to bring Emily and Ben along on their trips. Arabella Valentine was both nanny and teacher while their parents were busy.

Ms. Valentine knew that Emily and Ben loved Sebastian. But she didn't know that he was real–at least to them. Like most adults, she didn't pay much attention to small bears.

A loud thump brought Sebastian back to the present. He stood up, trying not to wobble on the moving belt. *I'll have to jump*, he thought.

"There he is!" said a familiar voice.

Suddenly, Sebastian saw light up ahead. Then–Flap! Slap! He was out in the open again.

"There he is!" said a familiar voice. Emily snatched him up. At the same time, Ben grabbed the suitcase.

"I wasn't scared," Sebastian told Emily.

"There was no reason to be, silly," she said. "The belt goes around and around. All you had to do was stay put."

"Oh," said Sebastian. He was a little disappointed that he hadn't been in any danger after all.

Ms. Valentine rushed up, looking grim. "Emily!" she said. "You must be more responsible. I can't believe you dropped your bear onto the luggage belt!"

"I didn't mean to get you into trouble," whispered Sebastian. "I'm sorry."

"I know," Emily sighed as she helped him into her backpack. "You always are."

They made their way through the noisy airport. There were people dressed in flowing robes and speaking different languages. *Egypt is going to be very interesting*, Sebastian thought.

Soon they were in a taxi. At once, Ms. Valentine removed her hat and ran her fingers through her frizzy, red hair. She pulled a sharp pencil and a small notebook from her handbag. Then she read for a few moments, nodding and making check marks.

"We'll look around the city of Cairo tomorrow," she murmured. "And, of course, we'll visit the pyramids and the museum. We have a lot to do while your parents are busy. There is so much history here!"

"What's history?" Sebastian whispered.

"It's the story of the past," Emily explained. "All the important things people remember. Like George Washington and the Liberty Bell and the Declaration of Independence."

Ms. Valentine overheard. "Yes, Emily, those are important parts of American history. But Egypt's history is much, much older." She went on, talking about pyramids and pharaohs and what life was like thousands of years ago.

Sebastian tried to pay attention. But he was a very little bear, and it had been a very long day. Before they reached the hotel, he was asleep.

Chapter Two
Bazaar Bargaining

"*I'll* do it," Sebastian insisted.

"Fine," Emily sighed. "Just don't make a mess."

"I won't," said Sebastian. He climbed up to the sink and stuck his canteen under the faucet. When it was full, he checked the floor. There was only a small puddle.

Sebastian got down and headed for the mirror. *I look like a real explorer*, he thought. His shirt and shorts were clean and crisp. His hiking boots were sturdy enough to tromp across any desert.

"I'm ready," Sebastian announced.

The words were hardly out before there was a knock at the door. Ms. Valentine entered. "Our taxi is waiting, children. We're off to the bazaar to do some shopping."

Half an hour later, they were walking through the Cairo marketplace. Throngs of people filled the narrow passageways. Men led donkeys loaded with bundles. Women carried baskets of food. Small children darted underfoot. Stalls and shops lined the street.

"Buy my rugs!" called one shopkeeper. "The most beautiful in all of Cairo."

"I offer the finest silks!" called another.

"Maybe I'll buy a souvenir here," said Emily.

"What's a souvenir?" Sebastian asked.

"It's something that makes you remember a place."

"Oh," said Sebastian. "Like history, you mean. Can I get a souvenir, too?"

"What do you want?" Ben asked.

"I'm not sure," said Sebastian. "Maybe something sweet."

Emily laughed. "If you eat your souvenir, you won't have anything to remember the trip by."

Sebastian sighed. Emily was probably right. Still, everything smelled so delicious. And it had

"Oh, that's too much," Emily said.

been a whole hour since breakfast.

"Children," said Ms. Valentine, "I heard you talking about souvenirs. Before you buy anything, you must learn how to bargain."

"What do you mean?" Emily asked.

"The shopkeepers always start with a high price," Ms. Valentine explained. "Much higher than they actually expect you to pay. Watch this."

She marched up to a stall and picked up a scarf. "How much is this?" she asked.

"100 Egyptian pounds, miss," the shopkeeper told her.

The bargaining started. Ms. Valentine offered to pay 50. The man said 80. Ms. Valentine offered him 60.

The shopkeeper threw his hands into the air. "Sixty, then! I am giving it away! You drive a hard bargain, madam."

"So do you, sir," said Ms. Valentine as she gave him the money. They both smiled.

"I'd like a bracelet," Emily said.

"Fine," said Ms. Valentine. "Just remember to bargain."

Clutching Sebastian under one arm, Emily walked up to a booth filled with jewelry of every color, shape, and size. She pointed to a lovely golden bracelet, and the shopkeeper named a price.

"Oh, that's too much," Emily said. Then back and forth they went, until at last Emily nodded and said, "I'll take it."

After Emily had paid for the bracelet, the man held up a necklace. "This would be lovely on you, miss," he said. "It is fit for a queen."

"It is beautiful," Emily agreed. "But I can't spend any more right now."

"Perhaps we could trade instead," the man suggested.

"Trade?" Emily asked. "What could I trade?"

"That," said the shopkeeper, pointing to Sebastian.

"No!" whispered Sebastian in horror.

"I'm sorry, sir," Emily said firmly. "I wouldn't trade my bear for a million necklaces."

The shopkeeper smiled and bowed. "You are most loyal, miss."

"Thank goodness," said Sebastian softly.

Chapter Three
To the Pyramids

"Can we climb the Great Pyramid?" Ben asked from the back of the taxi. It was another bright, hot morning–their third day in Egypt. This time, they were headed for the pyramids.

"You mean 'May we,'" said Ms. Valentine.

"Okay," sighed Ben. "*May* we climb a pyramid?"

"No," said Ms. Valentine. "At one time, it was allowed. But now it is not. Climbers were damaging the stones."

"That's too bad," Ben sighed in disappointment. Sebastian felt the same way. He liked climbing.

A few minutes later, Ms. Valentine spoke again. "Look out the windows, children."

Sebastian looked, too. In the distance, three sharp peaks poked into the sky. "Are those mountains?" he asked.

"No, silly," said Emily. "Those are pyramids."

"Stay with me," ordered Ms. Valentine as they left the taxi. She paid the driver, then led the way to the tallest of the pyramids.

"This is the Great Pyramid," Ms. Valentine told them. "It is more than 4,000 years old. It was built with more than two million blocks of stone."

Sebastian wondered how anyone had ever counted all those stones. He usually had trouble once he got past 44.

They joined a tour group. As the guide led them around the base of the pyramid, he talked about the pharaoh or king who had been buried there. He also talked about how many workers it had taken to build the pyramid, and how they had moved the stone blocks.

"Now we'll go inside," said Ms. Valentine

when the tour ended. “We have special tickets for that.”

Another guide motioned them through the entrance. The air inside was hot, still, and stuffy. To Sebastian, it seemed like all they did for the next hour was climb. The farther up they went, the narrower the passages became.

Sebastian wasn’t sure he liked being inside a pyramid. So he started to whistle a cheery little tune to take his mind off the blank stone walls.

“Benjamin,” called Ms. Valentine over her shoulder, “please don’t whistle.”

“Sorry, Ms. Valentine,” Ben sighed. He turned to give Sebastian a long, dark look.

Finally, the passage opened up into a wide space. “This is the King’s Chamber,” the guide announced.

Sebastian poked his head up over Emily’s shoulder. “Can I get down now?” he asked.

“If you’ll be good.”

“I will,” promised the little bear.

Sebastian wandered over to one side of the chamber. He had an idea. He’d make a picture! He didn’t have a pencil in his backpack, but he did have a sharp stone he’d found outside. He was sure he could use it to scratch a picture into the wall.

For a few moments, he thought about what to draw. Maybe he would start with his name. Then everyone would know he was the artist.

He lifted the stone. But before he could make a mark, he was yanked off his feet.

"Sebastian!" said Emily in a fierce whisper. "What are you doing?"

"Making a picture," he explained. "These walls are boring."

Emily shook her head. "You can't do anything to change the pyramids. They've always looked this way."

"But–"

"Put it away," Emily ordered.

Sebastian put the stone back. With a sigh, he climbed back into Emily's backpack.

Later, they visited several other pyramids. These were some of the oldest pyramids in Egypt, Ms. Valentine had told them. To Sebastian's relief, they stayed outside. Then, late in the afternoon, Ms. Valentine announced, "Next is the Sphinx."

"What stinks?" Sebastian asked.

"Sphinx, not stinks," Emily explained. "It's an

"Sebastian!" said Emily in a fierce whisper.

old statue with a man's head and a lion's body." When they reached the Sphinx, Sebastian was amazed. The statue was huge. The little bear wiggled with excitement. "You can put me down!" he exclaimed.

"Be good," Emily warned as she placed him on the sandy ground.

Sebastian studied the Sphinx, thinking that a bear would make an even better statue. He got down on all fours. He stretched his back paws one way and his front paws the other.

"What are you doing?" Ben asked.

"Practicing."

"For what?"

"For being a statue," the little bear explained.

Emily smiled. "I like you better stuffed."

"Thanks," Sebastian sighed. But what he thought was this: *Is a small, stuffed bear important enough to be remembered forever? Like the Sphinx?*

Probably not, he decided sadly.

Chapter Four
Museum Marvels

"The Sphinx was cool," Ben said as they got into another taxi. "But it's too bad its nose is missing."

"Did soldiers really use it for target practice?" Sebastian asked Emily.

"That's what the guide said," Emily replied.

Ms. Valentine wasn't listening. She had pulled her schedule out of her handbag and was looking it over.

"Where are we going next?" Emily asked.

"To the Egyptian Museum to see mummies and other treasures."

A short ride took them back to Cairo. Soon they had their tickets and guidebook and were inside the museum.

They looked at jewelry and crowns, toys and games, chairs and tables. All of it had been buried with the great pharaohs of Egypt, Ms. Valentine told the children.

"Why?" Ben asked.

"The ancient Egyptians believed they would need their belongings in another life," Ms. Valentine explained. "And we are lucky that they did, because now we have so much to remember them by."

Eventually, they headed upstairs. "Now we'll see the most important display at all," Ms. Valentine announced. "The Tutankhamen Gallery."

"I know who Tutankhamen was!" Emily cried in excitement. "He was the boy king."

"You're right, Emily," Ms. Valentine said. "Tut, as he is called, was a pharaoh when he was a child and died when he was a teenager."

At the top of the stairs, Ms. Valentine paused, "But there's one thing I want to show you first," she said. She headed for a slab of stone.

Why does she want us to see a rock? Sebastian wondered.

When they got closer, he could see that the stone was covered with strange symbols. "Someone drew pictures on it," he told Emily. "Like I wanted to draw inside the pyramid."

"Shhh," she said. "Listen."

"This is a copy of the Rosetta stone," Ms. Valentine was explaining. "As you can see, there are three different kings of writing. The same story is written on the stone in three different alphabets. Archaeologists already knew two of them. So they used the stone like a decoder ring to read the third one–the hieroglyphs."

"Are these pictures really writing?" Sebastian asked.

"Yes," Emily replied.

"That's a good idea," he said. Whenever Sebastian tried to write, some letters always got in the wrong place. Maybe picture writing would be easier.

They left the Rosetta stone and entered Tutankhamen's Gallery. Ms. Valentine talked about the man who had become famous for

Sebastian could hardly take his eyes off the mask.

finding the tomb. She explained that Tut's tomb had never been robbed, as most tombs had.

"That's why it is so important," she said. "When it was opened, all the treasures were still inside. Not only that, but everything from Tut's tomb is now in Egyptian museums."

"Isn't that where it all should be?" Emily asked.

"Yes," Ms. Valentine agreed. "But at one time, objects from tombs were sold to collectors in other countries. Egypt lost many treasures before people realized how wrong that was. Now all discoveries must stay here, where they belong."

"Look!" cried Ben, pointing to a golden mask.

"Is that real gold?" Emily asked.

"It certainly is," said Ms. Valentine.

Sebastian could hardly take his eyes off the mask. It was decorated with jewels and colored glass that sparkled in the light. He couldn't help but imagine how exciting it must have been to discover the mask.

He wished he had been the one to find it.

Chapter Five
Desert Adventure

"Are we really going to sleep in a tent tonight?" Sebastian asked for the fourth time. He was sitting between Emily and Ben in a very small plane.

"We really are," said Ben. "In a desert camp."

"And we're going to ride camels, too," Emily added.

Sebastian shivered with excitement. He felt like a real explorer, heading off into the unknown. Maybe he would make a great discovery in the desert. Maybe he'd find a tomb like King Tut's–full of treasures. In his mind, he could see the headlines: *Bear Makes Great Discovery*! He'd be famous. Everyone would remember him.

He was still daydreaming when the small plane landed.

Inside the airport, Ms. Valentine pulled out her notebook. "Before we head for town, let's check that we have everything," she said. She began reading from her list.

"Backpacks?"

"Yes," said Emily.

"Yes," said Ben.

"Yes," said Sebastian.

"One yes is quite enough, Benjamin," Ms. Valentine said without looking up. She went on: "Sunglasses . . . sunscreen . . . hats . . . jackets . . . bedrolls . . ."

Emily and Ben answered yes to each item. Sebastian just nodded. He didn't want Ben to get in trouble again.

"Very well," Ms. Valentine said at last. "Let's find our guide."

The walk to town wasn't long, but it was hot. Sebastian swiped a paw across his face. It was hard being a very furry bear in a very warm place.

"There are the camels!" cried Ben.

The great beasts looked bored. Their eyes were

half-closed. Their jaws were moving slowly, as if they were chewing on wads of bubble gum.

The children and Sebastian waited near the camels while Ms. Valentine talked to Ameer, their guide. Sebastian counted quietly: "1, 2, 3, 4..." Then he counted again: "1, 2, 3, 4..."

"What are you doing?" Emily asked.

"Counting camels," said Sebastian. "There's one for Ameer–and three more. But there are four of us. Where is my camel?"

"You'll ride with me," said Emily.

"Oh." Sebastian was disappointed. He had pictured himself riding across the desert on his own camel–not sitting in Emily's lap.

Ms. Valentine and Ameer walked over. "Are you ready?" the guide asked in English.

"Yes!" cried Emily and Ben together.

Ameer gave an order in his own language. The camels grumbled and slowly sank to the ground.

Ameer helped the others, then climbed up on a camel himself. He gave another command, and the beasts rose to their feet. Sebastian grabbed hold of Emily as the camel rocked back and forth beneath them.

"Yala," Ameer said to his camel. Riding single file, the group headed out into the desert.

An hour later, Sebastian was sure about one thing: A camel wasn't the most comfortable ride. He slipped and slid on the creature's great hump. And its coat was rough and scratchy. Sebastian was happy when at last he could see something on the horizon.

"The tents," called Ameer. "We are almost there."

When they arrived, the camels sank to the ground again. Men, women, and children came out to greet their visitors. All wore loose, flowing robes. They smiled and said hello. Or at least that's what Sebastian thought they said. They weren't speaking English, so he wasn't sure.

As Ameer led the way to the tents, Sebastian suddenly realized he didn't have his backpack. He had dropped it while getting off the camel. Now he hurried back for it.

"What are you?" asked a deep voice.

Sebastian looked up–and up–and up! Even sitting, the camel was much taller than he was. "What do you mean?" he asked.

The camel chewed thoughtfully before answering. "You look like an animal," he said at last. "But you don't smell. What are you? Are you real?"

"I'm a bear," replied Sebastian. "And I'm real to Emily and Ben." Then he added, "Anyway, I don't want to smell." What he didn't say was that the camel *did* smell. And it wasn't an especially pleasant smell, either.

"We don't get many bears here," said the camel. "Welcome."

"Thanks. I'm Sebastian, by the way. What's

your name?"

"Omar," replied the camel. Then he closed his eyes and went back to his chewing.

"Sebastian! I almost forgot you!" Emily swooped Sebastian and his backpack into her arms. "Come on. Ameer's going to show us around."

There wasn't a lot to see. Seven large tents sat on the rocky ground. Six housed one family each, Ameer explained, and the seventh was for their guests.

Off to one side, a herd of goats grazed on the little bit of grass that grew there. When the grass was gone, Ameer said, the goats and the people would move to a new spot.

The afternoon passed quickly. As the sun dropped lower in the sky, the air got chilly. Everyone gathered around a blazing fire to eat. Emily offered Sebastian a bite of everything–meat grilled on a stick, a paste made of beans, and other foods he had never tasted before.

At last, it was time for bed. Sebastian placed his bedroll next to Emily's, then crawled in. Before long, he could tell that she was asleep. So were Ben and Ms. Valentine.

But Sebastian couldn't sleep. After tossing and turning for an hour, the little bear eased out of his bedroll. He rummaged around, looking for the Egyptian robe Emily had bought for him at the bazaar. Then he slipped it on and went outside.

The sky was lit by thousands of stars–more stars than Sebastian had ever seen before. He shivered in the cool air, grateful for the robe–and for his thick fur. Then he set out.

Sebastian hadn't intended to go far. But once he started walking, he started thinking. He thought about masks and mummies. He thought about King Tut and treasures. He thought about what wonderful thing he might do to be remembered.

Suddenly, Sebastian heard the swish of wings. Something swooped down, almost touching his head. Sebastian took off, running wildly over hills of sand and piles of pebbles.

At last, he stopped, gasping for breath. Whatever had attacked him was gone. But he had no idea where he was. He looked one way, then another. He was lost. Lost and alone at night in the desert.

Terrified, Sebastian curled up into a furry ball.

Maybe no one will notice me, he thought. *At least no one who swoops down on little bears in the dark*.

It seemed like hours that Sebastian huddled there. He could hear small sounds–slithers and rustles and flaps. Then he heard a BIG sound: THUD! THUD! THUD!

Something was clumping across the sand. It was coming straight at him! He held his breath.

"Sebastian?" called a gruff voice.

"Wh-wh-who is it?" Sebastian uncurled himself and looked in the direction of the voice. In the dim light, he saw the blurry outline of a camel.

"Omar!" he cried. "You found me!"

"Were you lost?"

"Uh, no, I was just out for a walk. I mean, yes. I mean–don't tell anyone," Sebastian said miserably. Then he asked, "What are you doing out here?"

"I came looking for you," said Omar. "I saw you leave. I thought that a bear who doesn't know the desert might need some help."

"I guess you were right," said Sebastian. "I'm sorry."

"Why?" Omar asked. "We look out for one another. That's the way of the desert. Do you want to go back?"

"Yes," said Sebastian in a small voice.

Omar knelt down so the little bear could climb up. Then they headed off. It was still dark when they reached the camp.

"Thanks again," Sebastian said as he slid to the ground.

"Don't mention it," said Omar.

Sebastian slipped back into the tent. In seconds, he was dreaming. He was riding Omar into the desert. . . . Two explorers off to make great discoveries . . . Two explorers the world would never forget . . .

Chapter Six
All Aboard!

Two days later, Sebastian sat with his nose pressed to the window of a train. Outside, he could see the silvery ribbon that was the Nile River.

"How long will the trip take?" he asked.

"About 12 hours," Emily replied.

"That's why we're taking a sleeper train," said Ben. "When we wake up tomorrow morning, we'll be in Luxor."

Sebastian nodded. Egypt really was an adventure, he thought. He had slept in a tent. And now he was going to sleep on a train.

Sebastian and the children were sitting by the window of their compartment. There was a bunk bed across from them. Ben had already claimed the top bunk. Sebastian was glad. He wouldn't want to roll over and fall out.

"Where is Ms. Valentine?" the little bear asked.

"She has the compartment next to ours," said Emily. "She said we should stay here until dinnertime."

Sebastian's ears perked up. "Dinner?" he said. "Where?"

"We'll eat on the train," Ben replied. "In the dining car."

"Do I like eating on trains?"

Emily gave her bear a squeeze. "I'm sure you do," she said.

Just then, the door swung open and Ms. Valentine entered. "Are you ready for dinner?" she asked the children.

"Yes!" cried Emily and Ben and Sebastian all at once. They followed Ms. Valentine into the corridor and toward the back of the train.

Sebastian studied the doors they passed. They all looked the same, like in a hotel. But the hallway of a hotel didn't sway back and forth!

Soon they reached the dining car. *It's like a*

restaurant on wheels, thought Sebastian. Tables lined both sides of the car. Silverware gleamed on the white cloths. A vase with a single flower sat on each table.

Sebastian enjoyed every bite that Emily shared with him. He also enjoyed looking out the window and watching the world go by. *I do like dining cars*, he decided happily.

After the plates had been cleared away, Ms. Valentine took her notebook from her purse. She flipped a few pages, nodded, then flipped some more.

"We have a full day tomorrow," she said when she looked up. "We're going to explore the Valley of the Kings and see some of the most famous tombs. There is so much to learn there."

Emily nodded, then yawned a great yawn. That set Ben off. Even Ms. Valentine struggled not to yawn. "We're all tired," she said, "so let's get to bed early tonight."

There were no arguments from Emily and Ben. Emily carried Sebastian as they followed Ms. Valentine back to their sleeping compartment.

It wasn't long before Ben disappeared into the

top bunk. Emily turned off the light, then snuggled with Sebastian.

"Will we see more treasures tomorrow?" asked the little bear.

"I think so."

"And kings and mummies?"

"I'm not sure," murmured Emily sleepily.

"And will we–"

"Sebastian, go to sleep."

"Okay."

Sebastian lay there, listening to the night sounds. The train went clickety-clackety. Emily sighed in her sleep. Ben's sheets rustled.

I guess I shouldn't have napped so much yesterday, Sebastian thought. *But I was sleepy after my night in the desert.*

At last, the little bear got up and walked over to the window. Outside, the moon drew a golden path across the river. A few flickers of light marked the location of a small town.

I could go exploring, Sebastian suddenly realized. *I can't get lost like I did in the desert. Not on a train.*

He dragged his suitcase over to the door, then

piled Emily's backpack on top. He climbed up, grasped the knob with his paws, and turned it. After he slipped out the door, it clicked shut behind him.

Sebastian looked toward the front of the train. He hadn't been there yet, so that was where he headed. At first, he had trouble. Whenever the train swayed, he stumbled. But at last he got used to the motion.

Sebastian made his way from car to car. There wasn't much to see except doors. There weren't even any windows to look out.

Then Sebastian's tummy rumbled. *A snack would be nice*, he thought. *I'll go to the dining car. There will be something there for a hungry bear.*

He turned around and went in the other direction, swaying along with the train. But when he reached the dining car, the door was locked.

His tummy still rumbling, Sebastian turned around again. He walked through car after car. He passed door after door. And he grew more and more worried. Where was his door? What was the number? He had no idea. He hadn't checked.

At last, the little bear was too tired to take another step. He sank to the floor and leaned his head against the wall. *I'll rest for a while*, he decided. *Then I can think about what to do*. He was upset. How could he ever become a famous explorer? After all, it was hard to find things when you kept getting lost yourself.

The train rocked gently. The wheels clicked and clacked. Sebastian's furry head slumped lower and lower.

* * *

A strange voice woke Sebastian. That, and being lifted into the air. For a moment, the little bear couldn't think what was going on. Then he remembered that he was lost!

And now he was being carried off! Was he going to be thrown off the train? Tossed in the trash? What if he never saw Emily and Ben again?

The attendant stopped in front of a door and knocked. "Good morning, miss," he said when the door opened. "I think I saw you carrying this."

The man handed Sebastian to Emily, who was rubbing her eyes sleepily. "How–" she began.

"You must have dropped it, miss," said the attendant. "It is yours, isn't it?"

"Yes, thank you so much," Emily said.

The attendant nodded and turned to leave. But just then, the door to the next compartment opened. Ms. Valentine came out. Though it was early, she was already dressed and packed.

"What is going on?" she asked.

"I found the young lady's toy," explained the attendant. With that, he smiled and said good-bye.

Ms. Valentine frowned. "Emily, you really must keep track of your things."

"Yes," said Emily as she gave Sebastian a long look. "I really *must*."

Chapter Seven
Sebastian's Fantastic Find

"Well, children," said Ms. Valentine as they stepped out of a taxi. "This is the Valley of the Kings."

From his spot in Emily's carrier, Sebastian looked around. All he could see was sand and rocks and sunshine.

"Where are the kings?" he whispered.

"They're all gone," Emily replied.

"Who are all gone, Emily?" asked Ms. Valentine.

"The kings."

"Well, of course they are," said Ms. Valentine.

"Don't you remember what I taught you? Many Egyptian pharaohs were buried here, but most of the tombs are empty now."

Sebastian couldn't see what all the fuss was about. Why come here if there were no kings?

However, once the guide took them into the first tomb, he understood. The walls of these tombs weren't blank like the walls of the pyramids near Cairo. Brightly colored paintings–thousands of years old–still could be seen.

"Wow!" said Emily as she studied a mural. It showed an Egyptian farmer planting seeds.

"Imagine," said Ms. Valentine. "This painting was made thousands of years ago. You can see how the people dressed back then."

"Look up!" Ben said a little later.

As Emily tilted her head, Sebastian peeked over her shoulder. The ceiling was bright blue, with animals and people painted in gold.

For the next hour, they moved from tomb to tomb. They made their way through narrow passages and stood in high-ceilinged rooms. They gazed at paintings of Egyptian gods, animals, and pharaohs.

Finally, they came out into the sunshine again. Ms. Valentine was talking to the guide and pointing to her map of the Valley. "There is one last tomb I want you to see," she announced at last.

The guide led them up a long staircase cut into the rock. On one side, cliffs towered overhead. On the other, the ground fell away sharply leaving a steep cliff.

As they toured the last tomb, Sebastian thought about the pharaohs who had been buried in the Valley. They had been important when they were alive. And they were still important centuries later.

That's how Sebastian wanted to be. He wanted to be important enough to be remembered for thousands of years. He wanted to be the most important bear in history.

If only I could think of something wonderful to do, he thought. He sighed noisily.

"What's wrong?" Emily asked. "Do you want to get down?"

Sebastian didn't want to tell Emily what he was thinking, so he just said, "Yes."

"All right. But stay close."

"I will," Sebastian promised. And he did. He

stayed beside Emily in the tomb. He stayed beside her when they walked outside.

"Do you want me to carry you now?" Emily asked at the top of the stairs.

"No. I can do it."

As he climbed down the stairs, Sebastian was still thinking about how to become famous. Maybe that was why he didn't see the rock.

"Ooof!" he cried as he tripped.

"Eek!" he cried as he tumbled over the edge.

"Sebastian!" cried Emily.

"Oh, no!" shouted Ben.

Ms. Valentine didn't say anything. She was up ahead. She was so busy talking to the guide that she hadn't heard a thing.

Sebastian rolled faster and faster. He squeezed his eyes closed–it was much too scary to keep them open.

THUMP! The little bear came to a sudden stop.

Slowly, Sebastian opened one eye, then he opened the other. He was resting on a narrow ledge. Above him, Emily and Ben were leaning over the side of the cliff.

"Are you all right?" Emily called. "Can you

climb up here? I can't come after you."

"I'm coming," Sebastian said bravely. However, when he started to climb, stones rolled under his paws. He threw himself against the side of the cliff and closed his eyes again.

"Come on! You can do it!" called Ben.

When Sebastian found the courage to try again, he saw something lying on the ledge. It was a piece of pottery. And on it were some strange pictures. Pictures like the ones he had seen in the museum.

Sebastian was excited. He grabbed the pottery, then glanced up. Emily and Ben were looking in

Ms. Valentine's direction. Sebastian unzipped his backpack and dropped the pottery inside for safekeeping.

Then he noticed another piece a little farther away. Very carefully, he started toward it. The ground slid under him. *I guess one piece is enough*, Sebastian thought. *At least for now.*

He slowly climbed to the top. Before long, he could reach Emily's outstretched hand. Then he was safe on the stairway.

"Thank goodness," Emily said as she dusted him off. "I was so worried."

"That was close, Sebastian," Ben added.

The little bear was happy to crawl into Emily's carrier for the rest of the trip down the steep stairs. He had a lot to think about. He was sure he had found a new tomb. It was probably one of the greatest discoveries in the history of Egypt. It was probably full of golden treasures. He would be rich and famous.

He would be important enough to be remembered.

Chapter Eight
Discovering What's Imporant

All the way down the stairs, Sebastian thought about what to do first. He'd ask Emily to call the newspaper. A reporter could write a story about his discovery.

Then he would go back to the museum to look at the Rosetta stone. He would use it to figure out what the pictures on the pottery meant.

And after that, he'd dig out the rest of the treasures. He'd need some help, of course. When the tomb was empty, he'd sell everything to the museum. He would be the richest, most important bear in the whole world.

Then Sebastian remembered what Ms. Valentine had said. The treasures in the tombs belonged to the Egyptian people. So even if he had found them, they weren't his to sell. He wouldn't be rich.

That's okay, he decided. *I can still be important*.

At last, they reached the bottom. Ms. Valentine and the guide were waiting for them. "Really, children," Ms. Valentine said, "you should have stayed closer. That trail is dangerous."

"We're sorry," Emily murmured.

The two adults walked off. But when Emily and Ben started to follow, Sebastian cried, "Stop!"

"We can't," said Emily. "You heard Ms. Valentine."

"I have to show you something. Something important."

"Well, make it quick," Emily said.

Sebastian unzipped his backpack and pulled out the pottery. Emily took it from his paw. "Where did you get this?" she asked.

"I found it," said Sebastian. "Up there," he added, pointing to the stairs. "And there's more. I think I made a great discovery. A whole new tomb."

"Wow!" said Ben. "You'll be famous."

"I know," Sebastian said modestly.

"We have to tell Ms. Valentine," said Emily.

"And the newspapers?" Sebastian suggested.

Emily ran down the path with Ben at her heels. "Ms. Valentine!" she shouted. "Wait!"

"Goodness, children," said Ms. Valentine. "It is much too hot to run."

"Look!" cried Emily when she had caught her breath. She held out her hand, revealing Sebastian's find.

Ms. Valentine took the pottery. She turned it over slowly, studying the pictures carved into the surface.

"Where did you find this?"

"Yes, where?" asked their guide. "You know that you cannot take anything from the tombs, children. It is against the law."

"It wasn't in the tomb," said Emily. "It was on the side of the cliff."

"What were you doing there?" Ms. Valentine asked in alarm.

Emily hesitated, realizing that neither adult would believe her if she told the truth. "Well–" she began.

Ben interrupted. "Sebastian fell," he said. "And when Emily got him, she found the pottery."

"May I see it, miss?" asked the guide. "This could be an important find."

Sebastian wiggled happily. *I knew it!* he thought.

The guide traced his fingers over the designs. "Hmmm," he said. "I cannot be sure. . . . Follow me," he said. "We will ask an expert."

In a short time, they reached a small group of men and women who were carefully sifting through sand and rock. A tall woman with short, gray hair slowly straightened up and smiled. "Hello," she said. "I'm Dr. Cookson, the leader of this dig. How can I help you?"

The guide explained, then handed over the pottery. Dr. Cookson studied it for less than a minute, then laughed. "It's a fake," she announced. "People make things like this to sell in the bazaar."

"Are you sure?" Emily asked.

"Quite sure," Dr. Cookson said as she gave the pottery to Emily. "I've seen enough old pottery to

Dr. Cookson even let Emily and Ben use a special trowel to dig in a pile of sand and stones the workers had already checked.

know the difference. Still, it's a wonderful souvenir. After all, you found it in the Valley of the Kings."

Sebastian slumped down in the carrier. He couldn't believe it. He hadn't made a fabulous find, after all. He wasn't going to be famous.

"As long as you're here, would you like to watch us?" Dr. Cookson asked.

"Why, that would be wonderful," said Ms. Valentine. "And most educational."

So for the next hour, they watched the team at work. Dr. Cookson even let Emily and Ben use a special trowel to dig in a pile of sand and stones the workers had already checked. "It will give you an idea of what an archaeologist's job is like," she explained.

By the time they left, they were hot, dusty, and happy. In fact, Sebastian had almost forgotten his disappointment.

But once they were settled in a taxi, it came rushing back. He frowned.

"What's wrong?" Emily asked.

"I thought I was going to be famous," said Sebastian. "And important."

"You *are* important," said Emily. "To me."

"I want to be important to everyone," said Sebastian. "I want to be part of history."

Before Emily could respond, Ms. Valentine spoke from the front seat. "Emily, thanks to you, our last day in Egypt has been our best. We got to help at an archaeological dig in the Valley of the Kings. Not many visitors can say that!"

Emily grinned at Sebastian. After all, he was the one who had actually made it possible.

"I also wanted to say how proud I am of you," Ms. Valentine continued.

"Proud?" Emily echoed. "Why?"

"You thought the pottery was real," said Ms. Valentine. "Therefore, it must have been tempting to keep it. But you thought about what I said about Egypt's treasures belonging to the people, didn't you?"

"Yes," said Emily, looking at Sebastian.

"I *did* think about it," he whispered.

"That's why I'm proud of you," explained Ms. Valentine. "You remembered something really important."

"Thank you," Emily said softly. She looked at

Sebastian and whispered. "You need to remember that you're really important, too. Important to me."

"I will," said Sebastian. But he still felt a bit sad. He loved being important to Emily. But he wanted to be important to other people. He wanted to do something that would make him famous.

Sebastian leaned his head against Emily's shoulder, thinking about their next trip. They were going to the Far East, Ms. Valentine had said–another part of the world with a very long history. Perhaps he'd do something wonderful there. Something important enough to become part of their history.

It could happen, he thought with a smile.

EXPLORING EGYPT

by Emily Parker

If I were going to live in another time and place, I might choose to be a queen in ancient Egypt. That would mean that I would be living between 2,000 and 5,000 years ago!

They were built by people without trucks or cranes!

Emily Parker's TOP 5 Best Things About Ancient Egypt!

1. ***The Great Pyramids!***

2. ***Their alphabet used pictures.***

3. ***Queens and kings wore beautiful jewelry.***

4. ***Cats were popular pets.***

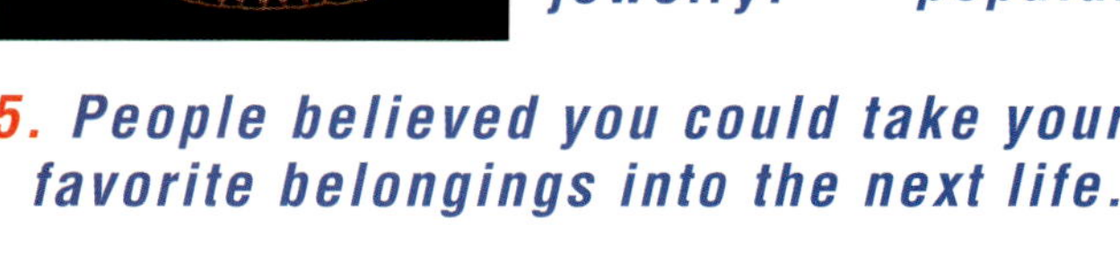

5. ***People believed you could take your favorite belongings into the next life.***

Egypt, or the Arab Republic of Egypt, is in a part of the world we now call the Middle East. Most of the country is on the continent of Africa, but a small piece – called the Sinai Peninsula – is across the Red Sea on the continent of Asia. Most of Egypt is desert – some places get only 1/10 of an inch of rain per year! It's so dry, sometimes there are sandstorms that blow for three or four hours at a time.

Pyramids: Math & Machines

So far, ruins of 80 pyramids have been found in Egypt. Some people think they're interesting because they were tombs for kings. Or because they were the very first buildings ever to be built with great blocks of cut stone. I think they're interesting because of math and machines!

Think about this!!

Sebastian says just thinking about it makes his head hurt!

How did the pyramid builders:

- Line up edges to be facing exactly east-west and north-south?
- Make sure the bottom corners were exact square angles?
- Match the angles of each corner so that the walls would be the same size when they met at the top?
- Move rocks that weighed as much as 80 tons up the side of a pyramid?

Scientists don't know all the answers. Do you have any ideas?

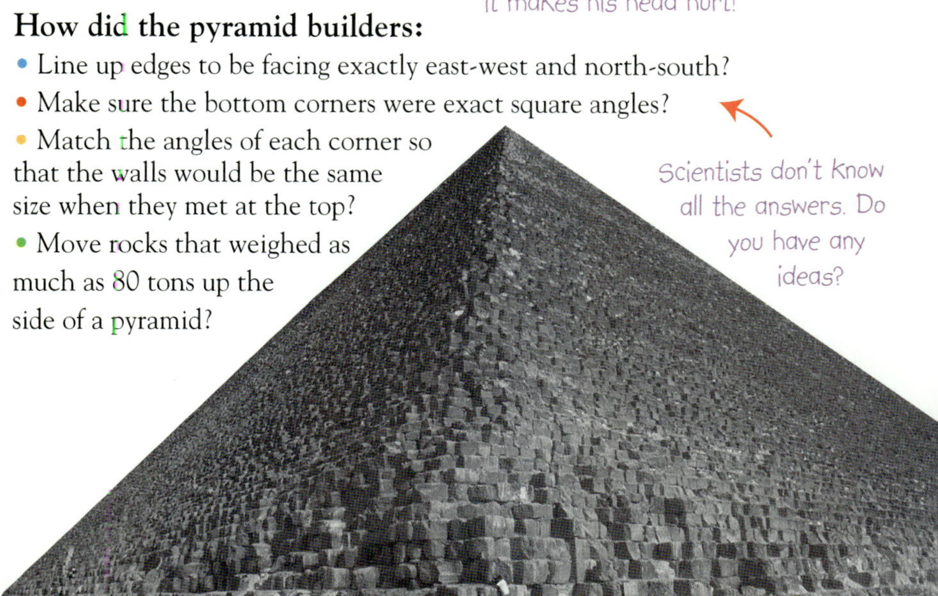

EGYPT AT A GLANCE

3000–2575 BC — Early Period

Egypt became the first nation in the world.

Egypt's first King, was named Menes (also called Namer).

First evidence of writing!

2575–2150 BC — Old Kingdom

The first pyramids were built.

The great pharaoh, Sneferu, helped Egypt become a great, international power.

His son, Khufu built the Great Pyramid.

2130–1640 BC — Middle Kingdom

After many bad years, Egypt rose to power again.

Many new pyramids were built in different places.

Peace lasted for 200 years.

1540–30 BC — New Kingdom

Pharoahs built tombs in the Valley of the Kings.

King Tut ruled from age 8 until he was a teenager.

The Exodus of the Bible took place.

Modern Times

Egypt was invaded many times.

Egypt became independent in 1922.

Sebastian finds a piece of pottery and almost becomes famous!

Part of the reason we know so much about ancient Egypt is because special scientists called archeologists have found so many things that have been well-preserved, such as pottery, paintings, and furniture. Archeologists study human history by digging up objects from the past.

Did you know that ancient Egypt –because of its long history– had its own archeologists to study its own past!

Lots of people think that hieroglyphic writing was a kind of picture writing. But the pictures don't stand for things; they stand for sounds, just like the letters in the English alphabet. For example, a vulture stands for the "a" sound. This special oval is called a cartouche and was used as a special frame around hieroglyphs for the names of kings or queens.

This cartouche says "bear."

Both men and women wore jewelry: earrings, bracelets, anklets, rings, and beaded necklaces. The jewelry was decorated with colored stones such as amethyst and turquoise, and made of copper, gold, and even seashells. Some jewelry had good-luck charms called amulets.

The ankh is a symbol of life and strength.

English has two types of writing

printing and *cursive*

Ancient Egypt had four kinds of writing during its history

HIEROGLYPHIC WRITING

SHORTER HIEROGLYPHS
called hieratic writing

demotic writing
for quick messages

Coptic writing
which used the Greek alphabet

M U M M I E S

The ancient Egyptians wrapped their dead in cloths and placed them in decorated mummy cases to preserve the body for the next life. Before bodies were wrapped, the organs were removed, preserved, and placed in special jars called Canopic jars. Archeologists have also found animal mummies! These animals may have been beloved pets, gifts for the gods, or food for the next life. Mummified cats, dogs, monkeys, and even a crocodile have been found!

Things to See in Egypt

The Great Pyramid

This pyramid was built more than 4,500 years ago. It's one of the largest pyramids. It's 450 feet tall and the size of 10 football fields! People who study Egypt think it took 100,000 workers 20 years to build it. It is made from more than 2 million stone blocks, which weigh thousands of pounds each!

The Great Sphinx of Giza

This huge statue near the pyramids of Giza has a lion's body and a human head covered with a pharaoh's headdress. The statue is 150 feet long and the paws alone are 50 feet long! Some people believe it was originally painted but now the color is gone. The stone has also been hurt over the centuries by wind, sandstorms, and even pollution.

The Nile River

The longest river in the world, it runs more than 4,000 miles through Africa. The Nile has been important to Egypt for thousands of years; it's been used for drinking water and crop irrigation. Did you know that the Nile flows from south to north? That's why southern Egypt is called "Upper Egypt." It is *up river!*

King Tut's Treasures

Tutankhamen is the best-known Egyptian pharaoh. His tomb was the first intact pharaoh's tomb that archeologists ever found. It was still filled with treasures and gold. Tutankhamen, who we also call "King Tut" and "the boy-king," lived from 1361 BC to 1352 BC. Another word for king, pharaoh means "the one who lives in the palace." People use to believe their pharaohs had special powers, like making the sun rise every morning.

Camels have always been important to the bedouin people who lived in the desert of Egypt. Camels can carry people and their goods through the desert for days without drinking water. Camels also provide milk and meat and their hair is used to make rugs, clothing, and tents! Did you know that camels sometimes lose up to one-fourth of their body weight in the heat? They get it back by drinking up to 25 gallons of water in just minutes!

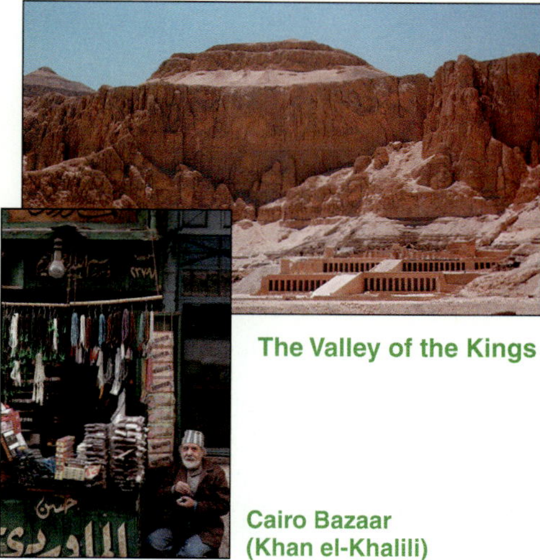

The Valley of the Kings

Cairo Bazaar (Khan el-Khalili)

Something You Won't See in Egypt

The Rosetta Stone

The real Rosetta stone is now in the British Museum in London. Like many of Egypt's treasures, it was taken from the country by its discoverers. Archaeologists and treasure hunters once kept the things they found. Today it is illegal to remove artifacts (objects from the past) from Egypt.

The Rosetta stone is very important because it helped people figure out how to translate the hieroglyphic writing in tombs. It was made around 200 BC and rediscovered in 1799. It has a story written on it in three different alphabets, including hieroglyphs. Because scientists knew how to read the other alphabets on the stone, they were able to figure out what the hieroglyphs meant.

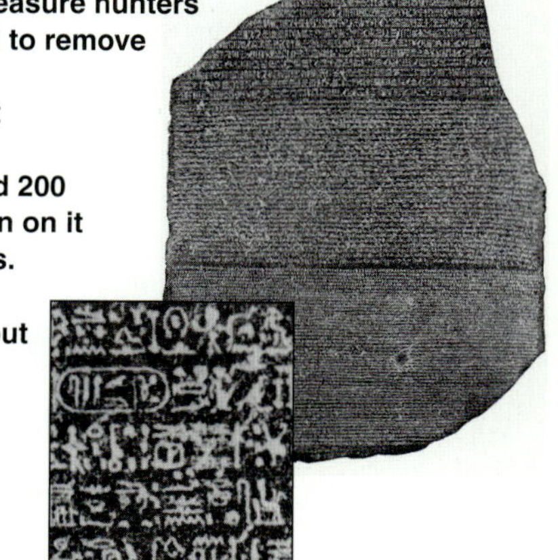

It took them a long time—more than 20 years!

Special thanks to Jill Ervais, for providing helpful comments on the *Exploring Egypt* section.

Photography Credits for *Exploring Egypt*

Page 52: Queen Nefertiti, Copyright © Bettmann/Corbis;
Great Pyramid, Copyright © Larry Lee Photography/Corbis;
Tomb painting, Copyright © Charles & Josette Lenars/Corbis;
Ankh collar, Copyright © Gianni Degli Orti/Corbis;
Mummified cat, Copyright © The Illuminated London News Picture Library, London, UK/Bridgeman Art Library

Page 53: Great Pyramid at Giza,
Copyright © Richard T. Nowitz/Corbis

Page 54: Workers at pharaonic underground grave,
Copyright © AFP/Corbis

Page 55: Gold ankh, Copyright © Egyptian National Museum, Cairo, Egypt/Bridgeman Art Library;
Sarcophagus of Nehemes Mentou, Photograph by Peter Willi.
Copyright © Musée des Beaux-Arts,
Grenoble, France/Bridgeman Art Library;
Crocodile mummy, Copyright © O. Alamany & E. Vicens/Corbis

Page 56: Great Pyramid, Copyright © Larry Lee Photography/Corbis;
Great Sphinx, Copyright © Otto Lang/Corbis;
The Nile River, Copyright © Dallas and John Heaton/Corbis

Page 57: Funeral mask, Copyright © Bettmann/Corbis;
Camel, Copyright © Charles & Josette Lenars/Corbis;
The Valley of the Kings, Copyright © Otto Lang/Corbis;
Khan al-Khalili, Copyright © K.M. Westermann/Corbis;
The Rosetta Stone, Copyright © Bettmann/Corbis

IF YOU ENJOYED this book, you'll find lots more to love in the Bear & Company catalog.

With a little magic and make-believe, even the littlest bear can do amazing things! A great family read-aloud. *Recommended for ages 3–6.*

Follow a trio of animal detectives as they solve mysteries in their forest home. A great choice for young readers! *Recommended for ages 5–9.*

Duke
THE BEAR DETECTIVE

Discover some of the world's most interesting habitats through the adventures of animals that live there. *Recommended for ages 4–10.*

A teddy bear travels the globe and finds mischief and fun wherever he goes. Lots of fun for chapter book readers who love travel adventures. *Recommended for ages 6–10.*

Three easy ways to request a free catalog

- *Mail the postcard below*
- *Visit www.BearandCo.com*
- *Call 1-800-596-4577*

Please send me a catalog!

I'm interested in: (check all that apply)

☐ Digby in Disguise ☐ My Home
☐ Duke The Bear Detective ☐ Suitcase Bear Adventures

Name ______________________

Address ______________________

City ______________ State ________ Zip ________

Email Address ______________________

Please provide email address if you are 18 or older and interested in receiving email updates from Bear & Company.

Send a catalog to my friend!

Name ______________________

Address ______________________

City ______________ State ________ Zip ________

IF THE POSTCARD below has already been used and you would like a Bear & Company catalog, send your name and address to:

Bear & Company
P.O. Box 3876
Gettysburg, PA 17325

OR visit us on the web at
www.BearandCo.com

OR call 1 800-596-4577

Stories to inspire your imagination . . .
. . . New friends to warm your heart™

NO POSTAGE
NECESSARY
IF MAILED
IN THE
UNITED STATES

BUSINESS REPLY MAIL

FIRST-CLASS MAIL PERMIT NO. 363 GETTYSBURG PA

POSTAGE WILL BE PAID BY ADDRESSEE

BEAR & COMPANY
PO BOX 3876
GETTYSBURG PA 17325-9924